Suspicions

A Play

N. J. Crisp

A Samuel French Acting Edition

Founded 1830

SAMUELFRENCH-LONDON.CO.UK
SAMUELFRENCH.COM

ISBN 978-0-573-01901-2

www.samuelfrench-london.co.uk

www.samuelfrench.com

FOR AMATEUR PRODUCTION ENQUIRIES

UNITED KINGDOM AND WORLD
EXCLUDING NORTH AMERICA
plays@SamuelFrench-London.co.uk
020 7255 4302/01

Each title is subject to availability from Samuel French,

depending upon country of performance.

CHARACTERS

Bill
Lucy
Tom
Kate
Taxi-driver (unseen)

The action takes place in the living room of a rambling Victorian house in a market town on the North Hampshire border

Time—the present

PROLOGUE

As the house Lights dim there is the sound of a telephone ringing several times. When it is answered the sound indicates that the caller is using a call box

Lucy Hallo ... Hallo?

Bill (*distorted*) Hi, it's me. You're back then. How're things?

Lucy All right. Where are you?

Bill On my way home. Come round in about an hour, OK? I need to talk to you.

Lucy I'd rather we talked here.

Bill No, make it my place. Explain later. Must rush. See you soon.

The dialling tone is heard as Bill rings off

Lucy Bill ... hallo ... hallo?

ACT I

SCENE 1

The living-room of a substantial, somewhat rambling, late Victorian house, in a market town near the borders of North Hampshire. A Saturday in November. Early evening

There are two doors leading into the living-room. The one to the left is open and leads into a lobby. There is one step up into this lobby area beyond which is a kitchen. Most of the kitchen, including the door to the outside, is out of sight. The only object in view is a very large deep freeze, with a top lid, placed end on to the living-room, in the lobby

The door to the right, also standing open, leads into the hall. Through the open door a large coatstand can be seen, and part of a door (never opened) facing the audience, which leads into a dining-room. The front door is to the right and is probably out of sight unless it is opened

There is nothing box-like about the rooms. Instead the house tends towards odd corners and nooks and crannies. The living-room is pleasantly furnished, although it should feel as if the furniture is not quite where it belongs, as though it could be more harmoniously arranged

Against the right hand wall is a large wood-burning stove. Set in the back wall is a large bay window, with the curtains drawn. To the right is a settee, awkwardly angled so that anyone entering from the hall has to skirt it. By the settee there is a coffee table, with an armchair on the other side of it. There is a small period table in the bay of the window. On it is a vase containing wilted flowers

To the left is a desk and a chair. There is a typewriter or a small word processor and a telephone on the desk. Against the wall there are well-stocked bookshelves and a drinks fitment with bottles and glasses. Another armchair is slightly in the way of the door

The Lights are on in the hall and the kitchen as well as the living-room. The kitchen light is of the fluorescent variety, cold and hard

The CURTAIN rises to the sound of a rasping, intermittent snarl of a power saw being operated off stage. After a while it stops

Bill enters through the kitchen soon after, carrying a basket of newly sawn logs. He puts it down beside the wood-burning stove and refuels the stove with two or three logs. He turns the control up to high. Bill is fortyish and good-looking in a carefree sort of way. At his best, there is a jaunty, likeable insouciance about him; whether this equips him too well to handle the harsher aspects of life is another matter. He is wearing a white shirt open at the neck, black trousers and black shoes

There is a polite knock on the front door

Bill (*calling*) Give it a shove.

Lucy appears in the hall, closes the front door and snaps the lock closed. She is about thirty, nice-looking, with open features, and a good figure underneath the heavy coat she is wearing

Bill flashes a smile at her

Say hallo in a minute. Hands dirty.

Bill exits into the kitchen and washes his hands out of sight

Lucy comes into the living-room, a little ill at ease

(*Off*) Been sawing logs.
Lucy (*looking round*) Everything's been moved round.
Bill (*off*) Eh? Oh, yes.
Lucy Why? It doesn't feel right at all.
Bill (*off*) Really? Looks fine to me.

Bill enters the living-room

(*Approaching Lucy*) Good to see you. This is the proper "hallo".
Lucy Well, hallo, Bill.

They embrace and kiss briefly with a certain caution

Bill draws back a little and begins to take off Lucy's coat

Bill Get rid of this thing for a start. It's like trying to cuddle an eskimo.
Lucy Are you sure it's . . .
Bill It's all right. Definitely. Bill says so. OK? There. (*He drops Lucy's coat on a nearby armchair and holds her tightly*) That's better. God, I missed you. I really missed you. (*Inconsequently*) Feel like a drink?
Lucy Do you?
Bill Yes. Well that, or take the rest of your clothes off. I could be persuaded.
Lucy I think we should have a drink.

Bill moves to the drinks fitment

Bill First, right? Very wise. Good thinking.

Bill fixes a Scotch for himself and a sherry for Lucy in a nervous and jerky manner. Lucy watches him curiously

Lucy Are you all right?
Bill Me? Yes. As rain. Or ninepence. Don't mind.
Lucy You seem a bit jumpy.
Bill Rubbish.
Lucy Tensed up.

Bill Sherry for you?

Lucy I can tell.

Bill I do wish women didn't have this bad habit of telling you how you feel. I'm fine.

Lucy I'm not "women", dear, I'm me.

Bill crosses with the drinks and hands Lucy her sherry

Bill All right, you're you. Here's to you. (*He drinks as for a toast*)

Lucy just watches him. Despite his denials, Bill remains restless, moving about aimlessly

Lucy Did you really?

Bill Did I what?

Lucy Miss me.

Bill I could have sworn I just said so. (*His movements have taken him near the stove and, absently, he looks inside*)

Lucy resigned, sits on the settee

Lucy Is it all right?

Bill Eh? Is what?

Lucy That object you're peering into.

Bill Oh, yes. Marvellous things but they don't quite burn for ever. Just caught it in time.

Lucy Oh, good.

Bill (*looking at her*) I missed you. I couldn't wait to see you again. It was the longest seven days of my life.

Lucy You made me go.

Bill I didn't make you. (*He resumes his prowling round the room*) I thought it was the best thing. That's different.

Lucy You're very good at that, aren't you. Persuading other people what's best for them.

Bill Would that were true.

Lucy But really you mean what's best for you.

Bill I certainly don't go around thinking, "I wonder what I can do that would be worst for me? Something really disastrous." Do you?

Lucy Sometimes it seems to work out that way.

Bill You go in for too much introspection. Anyway, how was it in sunny Lincoln?

Lucy Freezing. Rather sad.

Bill Sad? Why?

Lucy My father pretending he was far happier now. My mother pretending she believed him. Sad.

Bill He should never have retired. Serious mistake.

Lucy He had no choice. He was told.

Bill Thank God no one can tell me.

Lucy You'll have to, one day.

Bill No. Carry on till I drop dead, that's me.

Lucy Even your eyesight won't last for ever.

Bill It doesn't have to. I don't propose to live for ever. (*He gazes up at the ceiling*) You hear me up there? You taking notes? Just long enough, OK? (*He finishes his drink and looks at Lucy's drink*) Ready for another one?
Lucy No.

Bill crosses to the drinks fitment and gives himself another whisky

Bill So, what did you do?
Lucy Nothing much. I was fussed over, made much of——
Bill There you are. That's why I thought you should go. Cheer the old folks up. And so you did.
Lucy Not quite. The same old subject came up, as usual.
Bill Not with you. What subject?
Lucy Oh, that I'm their only offspring and high time they became grand-parents. That sort of thing.
Bill You never know. You might be able to oblige them one fine day after all.
Lucy Hardly. (*She finishes her drink and puts it down*)
Bill (*indicating her glass*) Ready now?
Lucy No.
Bill Something else? Gin? Scotch? Martini? Glass of wine?
Lucy Bill, another drink won't make it any easier.
Bill Make what?
Lucy That week away from you, I had plenty of time to do some thinking. And the more I thought about it, the way you'd jumped at it when I told you my mother wanted me to go and stay, as if you'd suddenly seen an opportunity——
Bill (*shaking his head; interrupting*) It wasn't like that.
Lucy You wanted me out of the way.
Bill I wouldn't put it quite like that.
Lucy Never mind the "quite". Did you or not?
Bill There was something that had to be done.
Lucy That's what I thought.
Bill Which'd be easier if you weren't around.
Lucy Yes. Sort things out. I'm right, aren't I?
Bill It couldn't go on as it was. Not right. Not right at all.
Lucy No. I suppose it wasn't.
Bill So. That's why I asked you round. To bring you up to date.
Lucy (*rising and picking up her coat*) You could have told me on the phone, Bill. I was expecting it anyway. (*She begins to put her coat on*)
Bill Where are you going?
Lucy Home. Before she comes back from wherever you've persuaded her to go. I don't feel like taking part in an embarrassing threesome.

Bill makes no move to stop Lucy

Bill She won't be back. She's gone.
Lucy (*pausing*) Gone? What do you mean, gone?
Bill Gone. Things thrown in suitcase, suitcase hurled in car. Gone. Left.
Lucy Left? You mean, she knows?

Bill Yes. She knows.

Lucy How? I run into her sometimes . . . She gives me a big smile, we have a chat, she's always nice to me . . .

Bill She knows because I told her.

Bill moves to Lucy now, gently takes her coat off, and puts it on the armchair

Lucy Told her what?

Bill (*about her coat*) You'll boil in this armour. The old stove's really pumping it out now.

Lucy The words, Bill. The words you used.

Bill That I was in love with you. That it wasn't a passing thing, it was for good. Etcetera and so forth. (*He puts out his hands, although not to embrace her. He places his hands on her shoulders, and manages a smile*) I didn't think to make a tape recording of it all.

Lucy What then? What happened?

Bill Kate isn't always all charm and big smiles. She can be decidedly volatile when crossed. She set a new record.

Lucy moves away from Bill and his arms fall to his sides

Lucy You mean you had a row.

Bill There was a good deal of screaming while she went for my face. If that's a row, yes.

Lucy (*about his face*) I don't see any scratches.

Bill I held her off. It was all very undignified.

Lucy She'll get over it. She'll be back.

Bill Lucy, you're not listening. It's all over. Finished. Done with. She's gone for good. She'll never come back.

Lucy You're not a woman. You might be surprised.

Bill She won't. Not after she's been told I don't want her, I want you.

Lucy You could have tried to put it more kindly than that.

Bill When you're being shrieked at, you get down to basics. (*He looks at his glass absently, moves to the drinks fitment and tops it up*)

Lucy Do you need that to talk to me?

Bill No, I just need it. It's been one long, horrendous week.

Lucy That's your doing.

Bill I know.

Lucy I should have been asked. Not told. Asked.

Bill Why?

Lucy Because I might have had an opinion, that's why.

Bill You might also have felt I was trying to off-load the responsibility on to you.

Lucy Instead, you do it first, and then lay it at my feet, like some sort of gift, an offering.

Bill I think that's a little unkind.

Lucy Moral blackmail. That's what it amounts to.

Bill (*tiredly*) Lucy, I'd got to the point where I couldn't go on. *I* couldn't. The way I feel about you, it just wasn't right. Seeing you as and when, being careful. There was nothing else I could do.

Lucy So what do you expect?

Bill Of you?

Lucy Unless you've got some reserve other women tucked away somewhere, yes. Of me.

Bill All I know is, I had to be honest with myself, and with Kate.

Lucy I suppose you thought I'd be pleased.

Bill If you're not, you're not. I took nothing for granted. Just the first, obligatory step. I'm single again. Well, bar the formalities.

Lucy Which will be legion.

Bill One in three marriages break down, these days. It's routine.

Lucy Bill, the break up of a marriage isn't routine.

Bill Well, enough people manage it. So can w——

Lucy We.

Bill I. Me.

Lucy We. If you're being honest and open with everybody, that's what you meant. We.

Bill How many lovers have you had since you were married?

Lucy One. You know that. You. Just you.

Bill You know me, what I am, what I do, what I feel, what I want. Whether you want me—well, you'll decide that for yourself.

Lucy Suppose it's no?

Bill Then it's no. Tough.

Lucy Yes. You could always get Kate back.

Bill No chance. She might as well be dead.

Lucy I think I'll go home.

Bill OK.

Lucy begins to move towards her coat

The telephone rings

Lucy Especially since that'll be Kate, and I'd rather not hear.

Bill It won't be Kate. I can promise you that. (*He lifts the receiver; on the phone*) Hallo ... (*His voice very warm*) Darling, hallo ... Yes, I've been away ...

Lucy her face tight, snatches up her coat

(*Oblivious; chuckling*) Really? ... Never mind ... What is it, your maths? ... How about some extra tuition? ...

Lucy's expression changes. She stops putting on her coat

Yes, of course ... I'll fix it, no problem ... Sorry, love, she's not here ... Don't know, gone off somewhere, you know what she's like, grandpa's perhaps ... You tried? When? ... and there was no answer? ... Oh, well, can't help you ... Are you all right for money? ... Sure? ... All right, sweetheart, love you too ... 'Bye. (*He hangs up*)

Lucy Sarah doesn't know.

Bill Evidently not.

Lucy She has a right to be told.

Bill Not on the phone. I'll have to go and see her one weekend, I suppose.

Lucy Will she understand?

Bill I think so. If I'm straight with her.

Lucy How? You're fed up with her mother, but you've got this other woman you fancy?

Bill She likes you. She said how nice you were.

Lucy Bill, she's met me what? Twice? Three times? Someone who appeared at her mother's dinner parties. What does that mean?

Bill Better than if she disliked you on sight, isn't it?

Lucy This is something else you've left out. How she's going to feel about it all.

Bill Time's on our side. She'll stay at boarding school for another three or four years. Time for her to adjust.

Lucy What about holidays? Take it in turns, with you and Kate?

Bill shrugs a "don't know"

You must have discussed Sarah with her.

Bill (*wryly*) Discussed? No, not exactly. (*His face, if briefly, becomes weary and drawn, the strain showing*) "And you can kiss goodbye to your beloved daughter, I'll make damn sure of that" is what she said. I suppose that was when it all went from worse to bloody awful. (*He sits on the settee*)

Lucy (*looking at him with compassion*) You look terrible. (*She puts her coat on the nearby armchair*)

Bill Sorry—nothing to do with you—had a long day.

Lucy Have you eaten?

Bill (*with a smile*) Sovereign remedy in your book, isn't it. Food.

Lucy It helps. You haven't have you. (*She moves towards the kitchen*) And now Scotch on an empty stomach.

Bill Hallo. A touch of the old nagging there. Is that a good sign?

Lucy No.

Bill Oh, thought it might be.

Lucy No, I'll fix something for you—before I go, that's all.

Bill All right. Thanks.

Lucy goes into the lobby and lifts the lid of the deep freeze

Lucy What on earth is the use of a vast deep freeze if there's nothing in it?

Bill Isn't there? Oh, yes, that's right. It needed defrosting, and a good clean. Must have forgotten to stock up again. Try the fridge.

Lucy exits into the kitchen

There is the sound of the fridge door opening, a pause, then closing again

Lucy (*off*) Bread, cheese, two eggs, cracked.

Bill Omelette and bread and cheese. Excellent.

Lucy enters

Lucy And long life milk. How can you drink that revolting stuff?

Bill It doesn't go off.
Lucy Bread, cheese and eggs do. Stale, mouldy, and smelly.
Bill It doesn't matter. I'll get a takeaway.

Lucy sits on a chair across the room from Bill

Lucy Why does everything have to be so bloody complicated?
Bill Nothing to it. Just decide between Indian, Chinese or a burger.
Lucy You, Bill. You.
Bill You told me you loved me.
Lucy That was a mistake.
Bill More than once.
Lucy Still a mistake.
Bill Was it untrue?
Lucy I didn't foresee all this—without any warning.
Bill I couldn't talk to you about it first.
Lucy I still don't see why not.
Bill Make sure of you before I did anything? Suppose you'd said, "No". What then? Carry on with Kate? It's not like that. There must have been something badly wrong with my marriage, or I wouldn't be in love with you the way I am. I want to be with you for good, but I had to be free before I could ask—if you feel the same. Or not.
Lucy Was Kate very hurt?
Bill Her vanity, mostly. May do her good. Perhaps she'll make a better job of it next time round.
Lucy You think she'll marry again?
Bill Kate? What do you think?

There is a silence

(*After a while*) Lucy?
Lucy I'm thinking.
Bill Oh.

There is a pause

What about?
Lucy Tom.
Bill Oh. Yes. Tom.
Lucy He's no fool.
Bill No.
Lucy He probably knows anyway.
Bill Has he ever brought it up?
Lucy He wouldn't. Not Tom.
Bill No. I suppose not.
Lucy But once or twice, I've caught him looking at me—that calculating, sideways look of his. Eyeing me—not that I've seen him much this last eight months.
Bill No, I wondered about that.
Lucy Nothing's been said, but ...
Bill He might not be too surprised.

Lucy Besides . . .
Bill What?
Lucy I don't think he'd mind much. Glad to be free again, I expect. Rid of me.
Bill I can't imagine anyone wanting to be rid of you, myself.
Lucy (*an inner sigh*) Well, then, I suppose that's it. (*She gets up and moves towards the chair on which her coat lies*)
Bill Sorry. What is?
Lucy I'll write to him tonight.
Bill You could always write tomorrow.
Lucy (*pausing*) I could I suppose.
Bill No hurry. Now you've decided.
Lucy No. Not really.

Bill takes Lucy in his arms and they embrace

Bill How do you feel?
Lucy I'm not sure. A bit frightened, I think.
Bill We'll be all right, Lucy, I promise. I love you so, I can't tell you how much. The hardest part—that's behind us now. Together, you and me, we've nothing to be afraid of. Nothing.

The Lights fade to Black-out

CURTAIN

SCENE 2

The same. Two weeks later. Late afternoon

The living-room is in darkness, with the curtains open. The wilting flowers have been replaced by fresh ones

There is the sound of a car stopping in the drive beside the house. The engine is switched off, and a car door slams closed

Bill enters through the front door and switches on the hall light. He wears a pilot's cap and uniform with four gold rings on the jacket sleeves and pilot's wings on the left breast. He carries a briefcase. He leaves the front door open while he takes off his cap and hangs it up, and parks his briefcase, his eyes on something outside. Finally he addresses someone outside, his voice raised slightly to carry

Bill Are you just hanging around or do you want something?
Tom (*off*) Want something. A word. Care to invite me in?
Bill Love to. Delighted. Be my guest.
Tom (*off*) Thanks very much. I'll come in then.

Bill comes into the living-room and automatically switches on the lights and draws the curtains, despite his apprehension. He moves to check the stove absentmindedly as:

A different car door slams and footsteps are heard on the path

> *Tom appears in the hall, and closes the front door. He is tall, in his thirties, well-built, a strong-looking man. His hair is short back and sides, his features even. He speaks in a slightly clipped way, his accent neutral. He has a military bearing but, by contrast, his movements are smooth. He wears a neat suit. His outward manner can vary from the apparently inconsequential to the abrasive. Underneath, there is an iron determination. Even when at a personal disadvantage—as now and subsequently—he never gives up*

Bill Feel like a drink?

Tom moves into the living-room and closes the door to the hall

Bill moves to the drinks fitment

Tom I wouldn't mind a beer.
Bill None in. Sorry.
Tom Then I won't bother.

Bill gives himself a Scotch, uncomfortably aware that Tom is more relaxed than he is

Bill Been waiting long?
Tom Couple of minutes. I knew you were on your way.

Bill registers this, but Tom does not explain

Bill Well?
Tom Yes? Well what?
Bill A word, you said.
Tom With my wife. A word with my wife.
Bill She's not here.
Tom Yet. I think you mean yet. OK if I sit down?
Bill Look, why don't you go home, and I'll——
Tom I've been home. House empty. Didn't feel lived in. So I thought I'd pay a call.
Bill Calls can be made by telephone. I believe that's what they're for.
Tom Wanted a word in person. Not on the phone.
Bill Let me tell Lucy you've been and she'll get in touch.
Tom Don't see the point. I'm here now.
Bill She's entitled to a bit of warning.
Tom You reckon? (*Referring to the settee*) Didn't this used to be over there?
Bill Yes.
Tom Thought so. (*He settles himself comfortably on the settee*) We had some good evenings here, didn't we, when I was stationed at Aldershot, looking for a little house not too far away. Dead set on a place we could call our own, Lucy was. We had to get on the housing ladder, she said. Before it was too late, she said.
Bill You won't lose.

Tom Oh, no, I shan't lose. Definitely not.

Bill wonders whether to challenge the double meaning but decides against it

Bill You can say it to me.

Tom Say what?

Bill Whatever you've come to say.

Tom Oh, we'll have words too, I expect. You and me. More than likely.

Bill I'm thinking of Lucy.

Tom Oh, yes?

Bill This hasn't been easy for her.

Tom Cries in her pillow of a night, does she?

Bill You know what I mean.

Tom What? Soul searching? Agonizing over the rights and wrongs?

Bill You may not understand this, but it wasn't done lightly. It took a lot of thought.

Tom Oh, I see. Thought. You're right. I didn't understand. I thought you'd been screwing her and she liked it.

Bill What are you trying to do? Make it sound cheap? Or needle me into a fight? Is that it?

Tom (*equably*) If I decide to take your head off, William, I will. I don't need any preliminaries. Nor excuses. (*Although he is sitting relaxed and not tense, it is clear that he could do just that*)

Bill loosens his tie

If you want to go and get changed, don't mind me.

There is no reply from Bill

That's you, as I recall. Can't wait to get the old uniform off and into the sweater and jeans. Go on. I'm easy.

Bill I'd rather be here when Lucy comes in.

Tom I'm not going to knock her about, you know. Not Lucy. (*Pause*) So, you chucked Kate out, then.

Bill She left.

Tom A dab hand in the kitchen, Kate was. A cut above the Sergeants Mess anyway. Quite a cut. You'll find Lucy's cooking on the plain side, I expect.

Bill Not especially.

Tom I've been thinking back this last couple of weeks, how Lucy was so taken with our new friends when we first got together. A bit dazzled, she was, you know.

Bill By what?

Tom Oh, Kate's style, the big house, your four gold rings.

Bill Nonsense.

Tom Oh, yes, felt we were stepping up in the world, being improved, you might say.

Bill You make it sound as if we were being patronizing.

Tom No one patronizes me, William. Two couples who'd become friends,

that's what I thought. I certainly didn't see this coming. Not until I was
posted. Then I began to think it might be creeping up over the horizon.

Bill So you weren't too surprised.

Tom That doesn't mean I cheered myself hoarse when that letter arrived.

Bill Tom, believe me, I didn't see it coming either.

Tom No?

Bill I thought of you both as friends. We often went to the pub without the
girls, you and me.

Tom That's true.

Bill Something happened. I didn't wish it, I didn't plan it. I liked you. You
were good company.

Tom You reckon we should shake hands and have a drink on it? Just one of
those things? If so, you're a real optimist, William.

Bill (*with a weary shake of the head*) You can make it hard, if you want to, I
know that.

Tom But you'd like it easy.

Bill I'd like us to reach—an accommodation.

Tom (*mocking*) An accommodation. I say. That's a good word.

Bill If you care about Lucy—you could hurt her, very easily, hurt her badly.

Tom I wouldn't do that.

Bill Say what you like to me. But don't hurt Lucy. Respect her feelings.

Tom You mean her feelings for you.

Bill Her choice, Tom. Hers.

Tom The trouble is, she made a different choice, nine years ago.

Bill It didn't work, did it. Or you wouldn't be here in my house now,
waiting for her.

There is a pause

Tom (*glancing at his watch*) Where is she anyway? Can't be at the office, not
on a Saturday.

Bill She'll be—here—soon.

Tom Home. You were going to say home.

Bill Yes.

Tom Hers? Her home?

Bill Yes.

Tom You won't mind if I check that out with her?

Bill No.

Tom Right, I'll do that.

With this, the heat seems to have gone out of the situation

*Bill visibly relaxes, and moves to give himself a refill. He gives Tom an
enquiring glance*

Bill Sure?

Tom Nothing for me.

Bill refills his glass

*Tom watches him carefully, but speaks in a different tone, as if it were a
mundane meeting after some time*

Well, how's business?

Bill As usual. Busy times, slack times.

Tom What about all those likely clients in the M4 corridor? Why you set up here, wasn't it?

Bill Oh, it's growing. Slow but sure. How about you?

Tom OK.

Bill Promotion?

Tom Offered a commission. Turned it down.

Bill Oh?

Tom Quite happy as I am.

Bill In the Special Investigation Branch.

Tom Yes.

Bill Still with the Drugs Squad?

Tom Not since Aldershot. Crime now.

Bill Much of it in the army, is there?

Tom Theft, rape, buggery, murder. All the things human beings get up to. Same as anywhere.

Bill Really.

Tom Get to liaise with the Kriminal Polizei in Germany—like our Special Branch—the Dutch police, the civvy Bill in the U.K. Very interesting work.

Bill I'm sure.

Tom Le Touquet, wasn't it?

Bill What was?

Tom Where you went today. Paris and then Le Touquet.

Bill You're well informed.

Tom Saw you come in. Watched you land. Then I came here.

Bill You just happened to be passing by? Or am I under surveillance?

Tom I looked up a guy I served with in Northern Ireland. Frank, he's in Security there now. He showed me round, hangars, everything. Very knowledgeable, Frank. It looked like the same plane you had before. Two propeller job. Piston engines.

Bill A Piper Aztec. It is.

Tom You didn't go for that bigger one you were thinking about.

Bill A Piper Navajo. Not yet. Put it off for a while.

There is the sound of the front door opening and closing

Lucy (*off*) Bill? I'm home.

Bill Just a minute, Lucy. (*He puts his glass down and moves towards the living-room door*)

Tom stands up

But before Bill can reach the living-room door:

Lucy opens it from the hall. She is wearing her outdoor coat and has a shopping bag

Lucy I got some . . . (*She breaks off as she sees Tom*) Tom. Hallo.

Tom Lucy, been waiting for you.

Lucy's eyes go to Bill

Bill He turned up a few minutes ago.

Lucy puts down the shopping bag, takes off her coat and hangs.it up, composing herself as:

Lucy You got my letter?
Tom Oh, yes. It arrived safely.
Bill (*referring to the shopping bag*) Shall I put this stuff away?
Lucy Please.

Bill picks up the shopping bag and exits into the kitchen

Lucy (*to Tom; moving into the living-room*) You didn't answer.
Tom Deal with it by correspondence? You should know me better than that.
Lucy You're on leave.
Tom Well I haven't deserted.
Lucy I know that. You wouldn't. No matter what. It wasn't a question.
Tom Had quite a bit owing. Took it.

Bill enters from the kitchen

We've reached an accommodation. Solves everything. An accommodation.
Lucy Meaning what? Exactly?
Tom Ask him. His suggestion.
Bill We behave like reasonable people. Discuss things in a civilized fashion.

Bill hovers uneasily near the drinks, his own glass nearly empty now

Tom (*to Lucy*) There you are. The exact meaning.
Lucy Discuss what?
Tom Things. To quote him. Things.
Lucy Sit around and talk about it? Hold a post mortem? No, thank you. Useless, pointless, morbid.
Tom I've been to post mortems. You might be surprised how much you can find out from a body—what it can tell you.
Lucy When it's lifeless, you mean—like our marriage.
Tom That's what you say. I never have.
Lucy It only takes one, Tom. One is enough.
Tom Well, even if you skip the post mortem, you've still got the funeral to consider. Arrangements. Disposing of the remains.
Bill (*to Lucy*) There are practical matters to be sorted out, Lucy.
Lucy That's what solicitors are for.
Tom I think it makes sense to see if we can't agree before we drag in lawyers with their bloody great bills. Or are you afraid of facing up to it?
Lucy No.
Tom Right, then.

Lucy sits, as does Tom

Bill (*referring to the drinks*) Lucy?

Lucy No, thanks. Not now.

Bill gives himself a generous Scotch

Tom (*watching Bill*) That why they kicked you out of the airline, Bill?

Bill What?

Tom (*indicating*) The booze.

Bill You know damn well why I left. I couldn't stand the bureaucracy, decided to pack it in and run my own operation.

Tom Yes. All yours. One second hand six-seater Aztec, and one old Cessna trainer. You still giving flying lessons on the side?

Bill What I do is really none of your business, is it.

Tom I hear running Air Taxis is on the dodgy side. People go bust. Your bank still playing ball, I hope.

Bill I'm doing all right. Thank you.

Tom I reckon Lucy fell for you the day you took her up in that trainer of yours. All those instruments, lord of the air, master of the skies. All that crap.

Lucy Crap is right. Post mortem crap.

Tom I'm right then.

Lucy He's everything you're not.

Bill That flight was nothing to do with it. We were just friends then. I took you up as well, Tom.

Tom Yes, but I didn't fancy you, William. Not like all those stewardesses.

Bill What?

Tom When you were on the airline. Pilots and pretty women, stopovers abroad, long evenings, nothing else to do.

Bill That's just a myth. It's not like that. Just part of the job.

Tom Part of the job? I used to watch Kate when you were reminiscing about old times. I reckon she thought it was more a case of you being on the job.

Lucy Was I your first?

Tom Don't be silly.

Lucy So what are you trying to prove?

Tom Prove? Nothing. Just reflecting, you might say. Like how he stayed a First Officer. Never got to be a Captain. Kept failing his command course. I remember him telling us that himself.

Lucy He also told us why.

Tom Oh, yes, how his Chief Pilot was a shifty bastard who had it in for our William. Personally, I always thought they got shot of him because he was a right piss artist.

Bill I never touch a drink before flying. There are strict regulations.

Lucy You don't have to defend yourself to him. Good God. (*She stands up angrily and turns on Tom*)

Tom (*remaining almost detached*) I'm just wondering if you've studied his references.

Lucy References? He's not applying for a bloody job.

Tom He's applying to take on my wife.

Lucy My wife. Your attitude exactly. A piece of property.

Tom I bought the property you wanted.

Lucy Yes, I thought you'd bring that up.

Tom You wanted it. My job to provide it. Also, my way of saying you came first. Understand that much, at least.

Lucy Really. And how's your German girl friend?

Tom Ah.

Lucy Yes.

Tom News travels.

Lucy One of your loyal mates thought I should know.

Tom I'm not a monk. If my wife removes herself——

Lucy My wife again . . .

Tom —you think I'm going to lie in bed alone and mope about it?

Lucy I didn't think anything. I only knew I couldn't go with you. Be a latter day camp follower. Not again. I couldn't.

Tom The house was to be a base, somewhere for leaves, for the future. That's how the idea was sold to me.

Lucy I know.

Tom Not an excuse to go on seeing him.

Lucy I know.

Tom Do you think you've been very fair, Lucy?

Lucy No. But now you have your German girl, I feel better.

Bill Have you two finished?

Tom (*to Lucy*) If it's about her . . .

Lucy It's not.

Tom It's day to day. She knows that. It could end tomorrow.

Lucy Tom I don't care. Any more than you've ever really cared about me.

Tom I always tried. I did my best.

Lucy Second best. Army first.

Tom The army's my life. You knew how it would be.

Bill Could I say something?

Tom No. You keep out of this.

Lucy Yes, Bill. What is it?

Bill I don't think this is serving any good purpose, do you?

Tom I want to be certain. Sure in my own mind.

Lucy All right. You offered me a bargain. You'd ditch your girlfriend if I give up Bill.

Tom It wasn't meant like that . . .

Lucy Let me tell you something. When Bill ended it with Kate, I was away. I knew nothing about it. There was no bargain beforehand, no each way bet for him. He could have lost everything. That told me more about the truth of his feelings for me than words ever could. That's the kind of love I need Tom. I always have.

Tom So it's Bill. For certain.

Lucy It's Bill. Come what may. No matter what.

Tom All right. That'll do.

Lucy Can I have a sherry now, Bill, please?

Bill Yes, of course. Tom? You know what I've got.

Tom No.

Bill pours a sherry for Lucy. He adds a dash of Scotch to his own glass

Practical matters, you said.

Bill Number one—divorce. We want to get married.

Lucy (*to Tom*) And I could divorce you, anyway.

Tom I've already worked that out, thank you.

Lucy Right. So that's settled.

Tom What does Kate say?

Bill She's agreed to a divorce.

Tom When?

Bill Before she left.

Lucy Did she?

Bill Yes. I told you, didn't I?

Lucy I thought it was all one terrible scene.

Bill Perhaps "agreed" is a polite euphemism.

Tom You mean she wasn't reasonable and civilized about it. Suppose she changes her mind? If Kate wants to be awkward, she can make you wait years.

Bill There'll be no change of mind, no need to wait. You can forget Kate.

Tom What about your daughter? Forget her too?

Lucy Sarah adores her father. We think she'd be happier with us.

Tom You'd take her on. Be her stepmother.

Lucy Yes.

Tom We could have had our own. I always wanted kids.

Lucy Oh, yes? When we were in Northern Ireland? When you were on one of your detachments without me, like Belize? Never settled in one place? Always packing up and moving on?

Tom Other people manage.

Lucy Children, yes. When they have one home. Just one. They know where they are.

Tom Children. His, you mean.

Lucy Yes. We talked it over, and decided——

Bill We want a family of our own.

Tom You've certainly done a lot of talking. Everything mapped out, all agreed.

Lucy Once I'd—accepted—how I felt, it wasn't hard. We want the same things.

Tom That little place we bought, it looks decent enough now I've tarted it up a bit. It should sell all right. Whatever's left over when the mortgage is paid off, fifty fifty each, OK?

Lucy I don't want anything. You keep it.

Bill Lucy, you're entitled to a share. It's your right.

Tom Contents, furniture, odds and sods, keep anything you want, we sell the rest, split whatever we get for it, all right?

Lucy Do we have to talk about all this?

Tom Yes, we do. Decisions have consequences.

Lucy Just do whatever you think is right.

Tom (*nodding*) Where will you live?

Lucy I don't know. I——
Bill Here. We'll live here, Lucy.
Tom Kate'll give it to you, will she?
Lucy What?
Tom She's entitled to her share. You heard him. Same as you. What's a house like this worth these days? A couple of hundred thousand? More, for all I know. Can you find a hundred grand to pay her off Bill? If not, it's sell up time and look for a cosy little semi. (*To Lucy*) You know, like married quarters.
Bill It won't come to that. I'll reach some arrangement with her.
Tom Suppose you can't? Suppose she's bent on her pound of flesh in one large helping?
Bill She won't. I'll work something out.
Tom You keep saying that, but we don't know what Kate says. It'd be a damn sight easier if she was here. Where is she, anyway?
Bill I don't know.
Tom She left without saying where she'd be?
Bill Yes.
Tom Well, where do you *think* she might have gone?
Bill Her father's or her older brother's I suppose.
Tom Before she left, didn't she say *anything*?
Bill Only that I'd be hearing from her solicitor.
Tom Have you?
Bill No.
Tom She been in touch with Sarah?
Bill If so, Sarah hasn't said anything.
Tom Oh, I think she'd mention it, don't you? Kate's dad, her brother, neither of them phoned?
Bill No. Why should they?
Tom Listen, if Lucy had turned up on her mum and dad's doorstep with a tale of woe about me, they'd have been on to me in bloody minutes, trying to sort things out. (*To Lucy*) Right?
Lucy I don't know.
Tom Yes, you do. Kate left, when?
Lucy Three weeks ago.
Tom And no word. Not about Sarah, nothing. (*To Bill*) That doesn't worry you?
Bill No. She could be in some hotel, with friends ...
Tom She could. Or something could have happened to her.
Bill Of course nothing's happened to her.
Tom How do you know?
Bill Because I'd have heard.
Tom Her car traced back here if there'd been an accident. Identification in her handbag.
Bill Yes, of course.
Tom You read the newspapers. Women get abducted and killed. They find a naked body. The car turns up in some lock-up months later.
Bill Oh, for Christ's sake ...

Tom It hasn't crossed your mind to report her missing?

Bill She's not missing.

Tom Then where is she?

Bill I don't know, and I don't much care.

Tom If it was me, I'd get on the phone to her dad and her brother, find out.

Bill Well, it's not you.

Lucy Bill, perhaps you should—I hadn't really thought until now—but three weeks . . .

Bill Because of what he says?

Lucy Just to make certain—you'll have to be in touch with her some time . . .

Bill Look, I've finished with Kate. If I never see her again, that's fine with me.

Tom I thought you were going to work all these things out with her.

Lucy Bill, just a couple of phone calls . . .

Bill I don't feel like talking to them. Is that so hard to understand?

Lucy But, Bill, think how awful it would be if something had happened to Kate.

Bill Lucy, I'm not about to make a fool of myself for him. Nor you, come to that.

There is a pause. Lucy is hurt. Bill shakily swallows his Scotch

Tom (*eyeing Bill*) You're not waiting for something are you, Bill?

Bill Waiting? What for?

Tom I don't know. You act as if you were afraid to make any enquiries until something had happened first.

Bill I'm not phoning all over England to please you. Clear? Understood?

Tom Ever read about the Setty case?

Bill The what?

Tom Years back now. A guy killed some woman, flew the body out over the North Sea in a private plane, and dumped her.

Bill What are you talking about?

Tom The Setty case. Wondered if you'd come across it.

Bill No. But I can guess what happened.

Tom Yes?

Bill They got him, because the body came ashore.

Tom Yes.

Bill Bodies usually do.

Tom We had a murder case recently. A squaddie knocked off his wife.

Bill Do squaddies have private planes these days?

Tom Not as a rule, no.

Bill Missed the connection there somewhere, then.

Tom He stuffed her body in the family deep freeze.

Bill What for? Cat food? On the thrifty side, was he?

Tom Once frozen solid, he could cut the body up with a power saw. No blood spilling out, that way. Then he could safely dispose of the bits. Got the connection now? Deep freeze? Power saw? Private plane?

Bill Lucy, I think your ex is deranged. Or he has a very strange sense of
humour.
Tom We caught him as he was sawing the body up. That wasn't terribly
funny.
Lucy You're not suggesting—you wouldn't—not even you——
Tom Just going on about my trade, Lucy. As usual. Nothing to do with
good old kind hearted William here, who doesn't give a shit if his wife is
alive or dead.
Lucy That's enough, Tom.
Tom Men capable of killing look and behave like anyone else. You could
pass them in the street. Or live with them. And never know.
Lucy (*low and hard*) Get out, Tom. How I ever lived with you—just get out.

The telephone rings

Tom I'll be on my way, then. Nice seeing you both.

Lucy turns away from Tom

> *Tom exits into the hall and out of sight, leaving the door to the living-room
> ajar as:*

Bill (*answering the telephone*) Hallo . . . Speaking . . . She's not here . . . Who
is that? . . . (*His expression changes*) Oh . . . I don't know . . . Why? . . .
What? . . . (*He listens for some moments*)

> *Tom enters during the above, and stands listening, shielded from Bill and
> Lucy by the half open door*

Where? . . . (*He writes on a note pad*) Yes, I will . . . Thank you . . . (*He
hangs up, shaken*)

Lucy stares at him, catching his—what?—fear?

Lucy Bill, what is it? . . . Who was that? . . .
Bill The police.
Lucy Not Kate . . .
Bill No—no—not Kate—but her car's been found—abandoned, the police
said . . .
Lucy Where? Found where?
Bill A garage in Ealing. No note. Nothing in it. The garage waited,
expecting someone to phone. No one did—so eventually they got around
to telling the police.
Lucy How long . . . When was it found there?
Bill The morning after she left. Three weeks ago.

As Lucy and Bill gaze at each other:

> *Tom goes out of sight and silently lets himself out*

The Lights fade to Black-out

CURTAIN

SCENE 3

The same. The following day, Sunday. Afternoon

The fluorescent light in the kitchen is on. The living-room is empty. The curtains are open, and there is a dull November light outside

There is the sound of movement in the kitchen

Lucy comes into sight there, opens the deep freeze and looks inside

There is a prolonged ring on the front door bell

Lucy closes the deep freeze, moves through the living-room into the hall and opens the front door

Lucy (*off*) What do you want?

Tom enters pushing past Lucy and goes into the living-room

Tom (*as he enters*) Thanks. I will come in, yes. Thank you.

Lucy closes the front door, and moves into the living-room. She closes the living-room door

Lucy Bill's flying.
Tom I know. (*He moves the settee a little*)
Lucy What are you doing?
Tom Wondering why the furniture's been moved. (*He bends to look closely at the carpet*)
Lucy You should try asking.
Tom All right. Why?
Lucy Kate threw a bottle of red wine at Bill. It spilt over the carpet. Bill tried to clean it up.
Tom What did he use? Bleach?
Lucy I don't know.

Tom sits on the settee, any half jokiness, half malice has gone

(*Ironically*) What now? A forensic examination for blood stains?
Tom Yesterday—I wasn't serious, Lucy.
Lucy What was it then? Your idea of a jolly little joke?
Tom It was—oh, I don't know. A mixture of bitterness and jealousy, I suppose. Meant to be a bad thing, jealousy, I know, but there it is.
Lucy I didn't think you'd care that much.
Tom Didn't you?
Lucy No.
Tom You were always the one for me, right from the first. I never imagined we might split up. I thought it was for good, you know, see through any troubles that hit us together. You didn't want a church wedding just so's you could dress up, I know. You must have felt the same.
Lucy Then, yes. Perhaps I did, then. But that's gone, Tom. Worn away. Just

being married isn't enough. Love means giving and somehow, you don't. Not things, I don't mean that. Yourself. You don't give of yourself.

Tom I know I haven't been what you wanted, but I did love you, Lucy, even if I didn't show it the way you'd have liked.

Lucy I think you've known about Bill for a long time.

Tom Not at first. I knew you liked him . . .

Lucy Later. I think you knew.

Tom Later, yes. I guess so.

Lucy You didn't come back then. You stayed in Germany, with your girl friend.

Tom Ah. So maybe you're a bit jealous too.

Lucy Me? Good Lord, no. Certainly not.

Tom Are you happy with Bill?

Lucy Yes. I am.

Tom No doubts crept in yet? None at all?

Lucy No. He's a good man, Tom.

Tom Yes, he can be a likeable chap. Open, straight, all that. But I've known others like him, and somehow I get the feeling that if things got rough, he could capsize. I don't know why. Perhaps there's a streak of weakness there somewhere.

Lucy You're doing it again, more of your cheap sneers.

Tom Not this time, Lucy I——

Lucy (*interrupting*) It won't work, you know. And you're completely wrong, as usual.

Tom Not always. Something did happen. Kate's car's turned up.

Lucy How do you know? . . . (*Realizing*) You were eavesdropping. Snooping.

Tom I was on my way out. I heard. Is it supposed to be a secret between you and Bill?

Lucy No!

Tom Is he worried yet?

Lucy Yes, of course, he is.

Tom And? He's done what? The garage?

Lucy He tried. Closed until Monday.

Tom He hasn't reported her missing though.

Lucy No, he . . . (*Breaking off and resuming in a flat tone*) That didn't sound like a question, Tom.

Tom It wasn't. I had a word with a mate of mine in the civvy Bill, C.I.D.

Lucy You did what?

Tom Don't get excited. It was only under the old pals act. Off the record.

Lucy How dare you.

Tom Dare do what, Lucy? Be concerned if a woman's alive or dead?

Lucy (*after a pause*) What did he say?

Tom Asked if anyone had tried to find out where she might be.

Lucy Yes, is the answer to that. Bill phoned——

Tom Her father?

Lucy Yes. No reply.

Tom Her brother?

Lucy The same.

Tom Did he try more than once?
Lucy Yes. We talked about reporting her missing but by tomorrow the
garage could have heard something—and her father and brother, they
could be away for the weekend.
Tom Were you with him when he phoned? In the same room?
Lucy Well, no—I was . . .
Tom Suppose you give them a ring.
Lucy I don't know them—I've never even spoken to either of them . . .
Tom You'll have to some time. It might as well be now.
Lucy I've told you, Bill phoned.
Tom So you said. You might have more success. Worth a try.
Lucy Are you implying that Bill didn't really make those calls?
Tom Lucy, I'm asking you to dial two numbers. If Kate's there, fine. So
what's wrong with finding out?
Lucy It feels like going behind Bill's back. Being disloyal.
Tom His wife has disappeared. He's tried, now you're trying again. Why
should he mind? Go on.

*Reluctantly, Lucy moves to the telephone, looks up a number in an address
book, taps out a four figure code and a five figure number. She holds the
receiver to her ear listening*

Tom (*after a pause*) Which one is that?
Lucy Her father. (*Pause*) He must be out somewhere.
Tom I remember Kate saying his health was poor. He didn't go out much.
Lucy She didn't say he was housebound. (*Pause*) Anyway, there's no
answer. (*She hangs up and looks at Tom*)
Tom (*about the address book*) The other number in there too?

*Lucy refers to the address book, taps out another code and number. She stands
listening to the ringing tone*

(*After a longish pause*) There's something else, Lucy. (*Pause*) It means
nothing on its own, but I wish Kate would answer that phone, and that's
the truth. (*Pause*) While you were away, Bill took the Cessna and flew it to
the Scilly Isles.

Lucy gives Tom a sharp look

Don't ask me how I know. He did. On his own.

After listening to some more of the ringing tone, Lucy slowly hangs up

He stayed overnight. Came back the next day.
Lucy He has friends there.
Tom Yes I remember, Colin somebody.
Lucy Watson. Colin and Jill Watson. They run a hotel there.
Tom Did he tell you he'd been to see them while you were away?
Lucy There's no reason why he should.
Tom No. He could have had a bad time with Kate, felt lousy, you weren't
around, decided to fly over and get smashed with an old mate.

Lucy That's how it must have been.
Tom I'm not saying it wasn't.
Lucy No. You're trying to make me think something's wrong—to remember that awful murder you brought up . . .

The telephone rings. After a startled moment, Lucy answers

(*On the phone*) Hallo? . . . (*Surprised*) Oh, hallo, I wasn't . . . You're not?
. . . why? . . . Yes . . . All right . . . (*She hangs up and looks at Tom*) Bill's on his way home. Some sort of engine trouble. He had to turn back.
Tom Forget what I said yesterday. Just what we know. Kate left. Her car's found abandoned. After three weeks, no one knows where she is. Three days after she left, Bill flew across water to the Scilly Isles. He doesn't report her missing. He doesn't want to phone around and see if she's all right. That's what we know. Is that unfair?
Lucy No. But there could be some good explanation.
Tom I hope there is.

Lucy gives him a doubtful look

I mean that. You're here. With him.
Lucy Oh, you're concerned for my safety now.
Tom If someone came to me with the facts we know so far, I'd think there was good reason to ask a few questions. I'd say it was a bit suspicious.
Lucy Yes, but you have that kind of mind. And you want to persuade me to think the same way.
Tom I'm asking you to look at it from the outside. If you can.
Lucy If something terrible *had* happened—a man wouldn't behave offhand, as Bill has. He'd pretend to be worried. He'd be *looking* for an excuse to report her missing.
Tom Apparently ordinary men commit murder—and then behave in a completely irrational way. That squaddie, there was nothing unusual about him. He spent too much time in the bar maybe; it came out he had domestic problems, otherwise a good soldier. But something happened and he went out of his mind. Until we'd put him away, then he sat in his cell crying. He couldn't believe he'd done it.
Lucy It's just not possible.
Tom When you came back from your week at home, how did he seem?
Lucy Oh, tired, a bit strained. Not quite himself. But that soon passed, Tom. Since then, he's been fine.
Tom What did you do, that day?
Lucy Talked—about Kate leaving—how we stood . . .
Tom Any more?
Lucy Not really. We had a meal—Bill fetched something . . .
Tom No food in? (*He moves towards the kitchen*)
Lucy A few scraps in the fridge.

Tom is in a position where he can glance at the large deep freeze

Tom Lucy, the police have to be told she's missing. Not sometime—today.
Lucy If we did—only that—not . . .

Tom Nothing else. Just that she's missing.
Lucy You go, Tom. I'll talk to Bill.

There is the sound of the front door opening and closing

Better still, we'll both talk to Bill.

The living-room door opens

Kate walks in. She wears a coat and carries a handbag. She is somewhere in her late thirties to forty, splendidly glamorous, elegant, poised, a little mannered

A moment of silence

Tom, especially, and Lucy reluctantly, have both pretty well become persuaded that Kate is dead. They stare at her as if she was a ghost

Kate gives her "big smile"

Kate Well, well, if it isn't dear Lucy. And Tom. This is a pleasant surprise. For some reason, I wasn't expecting to find you two here.
Tom No, well—somehow we weren't expecting to see you either, Kate.

Black-out

ACT II

SCENE 1

The same. A few moments later

Kate takes off her coat and hangs it up in the hall. She hangs her handbag on another peg

Lucy gives Tom a decidedly nasty look

Tom (*shrugging; quietly*) Seems we got it wrong.
Lucy (*quietly*) We?! ... You—you evil-minded bastard ...

Kate comes into the living-room. She closes the living-room door

Kate Sorry? You were saying?
Lucy Nothing.
Tom You're all right then, Kate.
Kate Fine, thank you. And you?
Tom Oh, I'm fine.
Kate And you, Lucy?
Lucy Fine, thank you.
Kate Well, it seems we're all fine. Isn't that nice. Are you on leave, Tom?
Tom Yes.
Kate Having fun?
Tom Not really, no.
Kate Oh, what a shame. (*A non-sequitur*) I'd forgotten what it would be like travelling on Sunday. Very tedious. Is Bill in the bath, sleeping off a liquid lunch, or out somewhere?
Lucy Out. Back soon.
Kate Ah, well, perhaps that gives us the opportunity to establish where we stand. Oh, I do hope you two are not standing on my account. Do sit down if you wish.
Lucy I'm all right.
Kate Tom?
Tom Me too, thanks.
Kate Well, as you wish. You must remember I'm not *au fait*, so you will forgive me if I'm a little tactless, won't you.
Lucy About what, exactly, Kate?
Kate I find you together, but in my home not yours, if you see what I mean. Are you visiting?
Tom I am. She's not.
Kate Yes. Quite. Thank you. (*To Lucy*) So you I take it, are now resident here, if I may put it that way?

Lucy You may, yes.

Kate My goodness, Bill certainly wasted no time in installing a replacement did he. (*To Tom*) I'm assuming you do know I've left Bill.

Tom Yes.

Kate Yes, of course you do. Your wife informed you of the new arrangement, and you decided the country could be defended without you temporarily, and rushed over to—to do what? Undo the new arrangement?

Tom Something like that.

Kate Have you?

Tom No.

Kate No. (*Another non sequitur*) There was no buffet car ˙on the train— naturally—and I'm dying for a cup of coffee. Would that be all right, Lucy?

Lucy Carry on. Everything's still in the same place.

Kate I rather meant, would you be so kind as to make it. Since you're now the lady of the house. I wouldn't wish to intrude.

Lucy does not move

Tom (*after a pause*) I'll make some.

Lucy It's all right. I'll do it.

Kate Thank you Lucy.

Lucy exits into the kitchen and out of sight

(*Calling*) You do remember how I like it?

Lucy (*off*) Yes.

Kate Black. No sugar. And percolated. None of that awful bottled stuff.

The only response is a certain amount of irritated banging of crockery in the kitchen, and the kitchen door being closed

(*To Tom*) Oh dear. Do you think she's annoyed with me?

Tom (*softly*) What do you think?

Kate (*softly*) I think she's a very silly girl. (*In a normal voice, chatty*) When did you arrive, Tom?

Tom Yesterday morning.

Kate The moment you heard.

Tom No. She wrote the day after she moved in.

Kate Which was when? I'm not aware of the precise timetable of events, you see.

Tom The day she got back.

Kate From seeing her parents?

Tom Yes.

Kate Good heavens, Bill was even quicker off the mark then I'd imagined. So you didn't rush over at once after all. Couldn't you get leave?

Tom It wasn't that.

Kate You preferred to be strong and silent. Dignified and aloof. Play a waiting game.

Tom I don't play games, Kate.

Kate No, I must say you've always struck me as a man of action. Physical, as it were. So what happened? Did being strong and silent become tiresome?

Tom I decided to fly over and sort things out. One way or another.

Kate Not with conspicuous success, it seems. Oh—that is on the assumption you still want Lucy.

Tom That doesn't arise any more.

Kate You mean you do, but she's not interested. Well, I'm sorry. Bill doesn't deserve her. But then, I've always regarded the concept of "natural justice" a dubious one. There seems to be precious little evidence of it in this imperfect world.

Tom I wouldn't know. I deal in man made justice.

Kate Like administering some on your own account, might you mean? You could, of course, easily. Poor Bill would be no match for you. You could reduce him to a bleeding, blubbering mess.

Tom I've been tempted.

Kate Should you succumb, may I be a spectator, please?

Tom If I succumb, I shall kill the bastard.

Kate Yes, I do know the feeling. Perhaps we should draw lots for the honour. (*With a glance at the closed kitchen door*) Lucy seems to be sulking.

Tom She's decided to let you get on with it, and I can't say I blame her.

Kate Get on with what?

Tom Your high born lady act. The one you put on like a fur coat when you want to be grand.

Kate Please, I wouldn't dream of wearing a fur coat. They're so vulgar— frightful.

Tom You know when you get like this, you remind me of those officers' wives, used to be secretaries from Peckham, and suddenly they sound terribly superior, educated at Roedean, with rich daddies in the country, don't you know. Come off it, Kate. You're just a jumped up stewardess who married a pilot.

Kate How very blunt you are, Tom, but not very perceptive sometimes. Put on, if you like, yes, but as camouflage. You know about camouflage. It conceals things. You're not the only one who's hurting, Tom. I'm quite vulnerable myself.

Tom If that's true, what's wrong with showing it?

Kate It's not my way.

Tom Then why go out of your *way* to tell me?

Kate Don't be so grudging. I confided in you, because, apart from being rather rude sometimes, you're really quite a decent man I've always liked—even if you are just a little bit of an inverted snob when it comes to officers' wives.

There is the sound of the front door opening and closing

Well, here's the master of the house himself.

Bill (*off*) Lucy, I'm back. Any calls? Lucy . . .

Bill enters from the hall. He is wearing his uniform and unbuttoning the jacket. He leaves the door to the hall open

(*There is a dying fall to his "Lucy" as he sees Kate*) Lucy? . . .

Kate advances to meet Bill with her big smile

Kate Will I do, darling?
Bill Kate.
Kate You remembered—how flattering.
Bill What the devil are you doing here?
Kate That's not much of a greeting.

Kate gives Bill a friendly hug and kiss on the cheek which Bill receives, stiffly unresponsive

Hallo, Bill my dear. How are you? (*She draws back a little and studies Bill's face*) You don't look at all well. (*Touching Bill's cheek*) Your face is quite drawn. Positively pinched.
Bill I'm not surprised. Excuse me. Must phone. (*He brushes past Kate, and heads for the telephone, taking off his jacket which he hangs on the back of a chair*)
Tom (*helpfully*) No calls while I've been here, Bill.
Bill Suddenly the place is swarming with uninvited people.
Kate (*to Tom*) He's just a teeny touch grumpy. Take no notice.

While Bill taps out a five figure number with one hand, he splashes whisky into a glass with the other

You might ask Tom.
Bill He knows where the pub is. If you want one, help yourself.
Kate I won't, thank you, Bill. Your lady love very kindly consented to make coffee for me.
Bill (*into the telephone*) Alan, Bill . . . Have you? . . . Oh, no . . .

Lucy enters from the kitchen carrying a cup of coffee, which she hands to Kate

Lucy Kate. Your coffee.
Kate Oh, thank you, Lucy dear. Most gracious of you. I am grateful.
Bill (*into the telephone; gulping his drink throughout*) Are you sure? . . . Yes, OK . . . Bloody thing . . . By when, soonest? . . . Right, well send a telex, say it'll be Tuesday . . . Blame the bloody weather or something . . . Yes . . . OK . . . (*He hangs up*)

Before Bill can take another mouthful, Lucy slides into his arms

Lucy Hallo, darling.

Lucy embraces and kisses Bill rather ostentatiously

Kate (*to Tom*) Isn't it romantic? Quite touching.
Lucy (*drawing back*) What happened?
Bill Left engine, sodding thing. Thrown a con rod. Completely buggered. Need a replacement.

Kate Won't that be very expensive, Bill?
Bill Yes.
Kate Oh, dear. I am sorry. Where were you supposed to be going?
Bill Sumburgh.
Kate Oh yes, the Shetlands, freight for those oil people. Isn't that usually urgent?
Bill Yes.
Kate Will they mind Tuesday instead of Sunday? Won't they be cross? Such an important contract. I wouldn't like you to lose it.
Bill Well, it's not something which need concern you any more, is it.
Kate Oh, I think we all have a vested interest in your continued prosperity, darling. I certainly do.
Bill (*to Kate*) I asked why you were here. Or have you just told me?
Kate (*eyeing the furniture*) I notice you've rearranged the furniture. I hope you won't mind if I say I don't like it much. But then good taste never was your strong suit. Although if it was Lucy's idea it's quite splendid, of course.
Bill It was to cover up the wine you threw at me.
Kate Yes, we did have our temper tantrums, didn't we. (*To Lucy*) I should get a new carpet and arrange the furniture properly if I were you.
Lucy But you're not me, Kate.
Kate No. (*To Bill*) When I left, I packed in rather a hurry. I came to collect the rest of my things. I hope that's all right.
Bill (*topping up his glass*) A phone call first would have been appreciated. Apart from anything else, there might have been no-one home.
Kate It really didn't matter if you were in or out. I'll leave my key behind when I go, though, naturally.
Bill Where have you been anyway?
Kate With my brother, mostly.
Bill (*to Lucy*) There you are. I told you. (*To Kate*) You nearly got yourself reported missing.
Kate Reported what?
Tom Missing. Police enquiries.
Kate Why?
Bill Why? You abandon your car, you disappear, and then you ask why.
Kate What do you mean, "abandon". I didn't abandon it.
Lucy It was found at a garage.
Kate In Ealing. That's where I left it.
Bill They didn't know who it belonged to.
Kate Of course they knew. I left a note under the windscreen wiper.
Bill There was no note. Why do you think they reported it to the police?
Kate I tell you I wrote a note.
Tom Perhaps it blew away, Kate.
Kate Do you mean to say it hasn't been repaired yet?
Bill No, of course not. They're not bloody psychic.
Kate Oh, how infuriating. I was going to collect it tomorrow or Tuesday.
Bill It's been three weeks. Didn't it occur to you to phone them?
Kate No, Bill, it didn't. I had more important things to think about.

Lucy We were really quite worried about you, Kate.

Kate That's very sweet of you, but I can't think why.

Lucy Bill didn't know where you were. He hadn't heard from you, nor your solicitor.

Kate I haven't spoken to him yet. Bill was worried? Were you, Bill?

Bill Not especially. Well, not until your car was found. It was Tom who kept on about it. He half thought you'd been murdered.

Kate Good heavens. How exciting.

Bill Yes, he definitely had his suspicions, didn't you, Tom. Bloody nonsense. I knew nothing had happened.

Kate Well, your instinct wasn't entirely correct, Bill. Something had happened. Although not to me.

Lucy What do you mean?

Kate When we parted, I was rather upset . . . I must have been—I don't usually throw things . . . Anyway, I just got in my car and drove off. After a while, I realized—I really shouldn't arrive without warning. I stopped and telephoned. A stranger answered the phone. An ambulance man. They were just taking him to hospital.

Lucy Your brother.

Kate Yes. Then the wretched car started playing up. Thank God a taxi came along. He took me to Kings Cross, and I caught a train.

Bill How is he?

Kate He's dead, Bill. Dead and buried.

Bill Oh. I'm sorry.

Kate Right to the end, I stayed with him. They did all they could I'm sure—but it wasn't a pleasant death . . . And then there was my poor father—I had to make sure he was looked after . . . (*An attempt at humour*) As someone said, life is one damn thing after another. Well, that's my three weeks. How was yours? (*Her voice is breaking*) Oh, damn . . . (*She cannot help crying*) It's talking about it . . . Ignore me . . .

Bill moves as if to take Kate in his arms. But, conscious of Lucy's presence, he compromises by touching her shoulders from behind in a gesture of comfort

Bill Oh, Kate, I'm sorry—truly sorry . . .

Kate We were always close, I loved him so much . . .

Bill I know. I only wish there was something I could do.

Kate Thank you, Bill. That's kind. But I'm afraid there really isn't . . . (*She moves away, blinking*) There. All done.

Bill takes Kate by the arm and leads her to the settee

Bill Sit down, Kate.

Kate sits on the settee

Would you like a drink? Brandy or something.

Kate No, thank you.

Bill You're shivering. I'll fetch some more logs.

Kate Oh, stop fussing, Bill please. I'm not an invalid. I've made an exhibition of myself, that's all.

Bill Just the same, it's not very warm in here.

Bill picks up the log basket and exits into the kitchen, out of sight

Lucy A fresh cup of coffee, Kate?

Kate Now that I would like. Thank you, Lucy.

Lucy takes Kate's cup and carries it into the kitchen. She leaves the door from the living-room open

Tom moves to Kate and takes her hand in condolence

Tom Sorry about your brother, Kate.

Kate Thank you, Tom.

Tom releases Kate's hand and moves to the open door to the hall and closes it. As he does so;

You're not leaving, are you?

Tom No, a bit of a draught, that's all. I think we want the same thing, Kate, you and me. I'm not enjoying this, but I'm staying. It's not over yet.

Bill enters the living-room, puts down the log basket, switches on lights and draws the curtains

Kate Oh, are we settling down for a nice long cosy evening? (*To Tom—as to an ally*) You may be right. Perhaps it's not over. We shall have to see, shan't we.

Bill moves to the stove and puts the logs in

Bill That's better. Soon burn up now. See about what?

Kate Arrangements, in the light of our new situation. Where shall we begin?

Bill Divorce, Kate. Start there. (*He picks up his glass, crosses to the drinks and refills his glass with Scotch*)

Kate I see. You wish me to commence proceedings.

Bill Right away. No point in delaying it.

Tom They're anxious to get married.

Kate What a very smooth and effortless transition for you, Bill. Will she have you?

Bill Yes.

Kate (*calling*) Is that so, Lucy?

Lucy (*off*) Yes.

Kate Just in case you thought we were trying to talk behind your back.

Lucy (*off*) I can hear.

Kate (*to Tom*) That leaves you.

Tom You know my feelings.

Kate You appear to be outvoted, I'm afraid.

Tom Yes. So far, I do, don't I. OK. Let's say I'll go along too, if I must.

Kate Well, wasn't that easy. We are getting along swimmingly.

Lucy enters with a cup of coffee and hands it to Kate

Thank you. Will you be starting a family?

Lucy I hope so. I'd like to.

Lucy catches Tom's stare, turns away

Kate But you haven't already. That's not what all the rush is about.

Lucy No. We're just very much in love.

Kate In the not too distant past, Bill was in love with me, and you were in love with Tom. Love seems to be almost instantly transferable in this little circle.

Tom (*with an ironic clap of his hand*) Well said, Kate.

Lucy Oh, really. Don't German women count?

Tom No.

Kate Men don't go in for that kind of simple arithmetic, Lucy. (*To Bill*) You haven't told Sarah, I don't suppose.

Lucy Why do you take that for granted?

Kate Because I know him, dear.

Bill That's mutual. I assumed you would.

Kate She's been acquainted, although not as soon as I'd have liked. You know why.

Lucy moves and sits beside Kate, her manner conciliatory

Lucy Kate could we talk about her?

Kate Sarah?

Lucy Yes.

Kate Well, I'd say she came under any other business, at the very least, wouldn't you?

Lucy (*with a glance to include Bill*) We've been talking about her future.

Kate Well, I think she's given up the idea of becoming a prima ballerina—

Lucy (*interrupting*) I don't mean that. Her immediate future.

Bill She likes Lucy.

Kate Does that remark have some particular point? I quite like Lucy myself.

Lucy Will you consider a suggestion, really consider it, please?

Kate I'll do my best.

Lucy I hope Sarah won't be too upset by what's happened.

Kate Oh, I think she will, you know.

Lucy Well, come to terms with it, anyway.

Kate She'll have to, won't she.

Lucy We think it might be easier for her, best for her, if she weren't uprooted. If this remained her home.

Kate You mean—you move out and live somewhere else and I live here?

Lucy No ...

Bill We'd like her to be with us, Kate.

Kate Oh, I see ...

Bill In a situation like this, there are no perfect solutions, Kate, but we honestly believe this is the best one for Sarah.

Kate Do you? Really?

Bill Trying to put Sarah first, her well being, as much continuity as possible, the only home she really remembers, yes.

Lucy Please think about it carefully, Kate.

Kate Yes. I will.

Bill I know it's a big decision. Take your time, as much as you like. Will you do that?

Kate Yes, I will. I'll take all the time I need. Which has already elapsed. No. Under no circumstances.

Bill Kate, please, at least try and talk about it sensibly. I'd rather not have to apply for custody, but if you force me, I will.

Kate Oh, don't be so ridiculous. I'd fight you and you wouldn't stand a chance, and you know it. You are not having my daughter. Never.

Bill Look, we're trying to be reasonable, to discuss what's best for Sarah. It's too important for you to keep saying, "no", without even giving some kind of reason.

Kate Oh, I have my reasons, Bill, but one will do. Contrary to what Lucy seems to imagine, I do not regard the ability to conduct a clandestine, adulterous relationship as a prime qualification for motherhood. (*To Lucy*) Your own brats, if you have any, you can mother them; my daughter, no.

Lucy recoils, gets up, and crosses to Bill

Tom (*to Kate*) There was no need for that.

Kate It put an end to a futile discussion.

Tom You're not so bloody perfect you can pass judgement.

Kate Oh, you poor man. You still care about Lucy. You don't like to see her hurt. Never mind. She knows where to find comfort.

Bill You said you came to collect things, Kate. Go and collect them. There's no more to be said.

Kate We haven't finished. In fact, we've barely started.

Bill What now?

Kate Your responsibilities, Bill. Sarah. I don't see why her education should be interrupted.

Bill No.

Kate You'll continue to pay her school fees until she's eighteen.

Bill Taken for granted. You should know that.

Kate Plus maintenance.

Bill Yes.

Kate And a reasonable income for me until I can find some sort of work.

Bill Of course.

Kate Not that I imagine there's much call for jumped up ex-stewardesses — (*with a glance at Tom*) with ladylike pretensions. But perhaps I can get a job as a receptionist or something.

Bill (*swigging his Scotch*) Anything else?

Kate Two former matrimonial homes. (*To Tom*) What will you do?

Tom Sell up, pay off the mortgage, divide up what's left half and half.

Kate Fair and reasonable. (*To Bill*) Can we agree something similar?

Bill There's a better suggestion which I think will suit both of us.

Kate Which is?

Bill Where are you staying now?

Kate At the house until it's sold. I'm an executor under the will.
Bill Did your brother . . .?
Kate Leave me anything? No. Sorry to dash your hopes Bill. It's divided between my father, various charities, and some in trust for Sarah for when she's twenty-one.
Bill Well, that was decent of him, very decent.
Kate He was always fond of Sarah, and when the will was drawn up, he assumed that *I* was adequately provided for. Whereas, and do please try and grasp this, I am an aggrieved wife of some long standing, with no means of my own.
Bill (*topping up his glass*) I grasp the point, Kate. No need to labour it.
Kate A better suggestion you said. Which is?
Bill You find a place you like, a small flat or something . . .
Kate I don't like flats, least of all small flats.
Bill Kate, be realistic. School fees, maintenance for you both, we're not dividing up a fortune.
Kate I'm simply saying I would prefer a house. A modest one. Even small if I must, but a house, if that's all right.
Bill Yes. Fine. Whatever you say.
Kate Although tasteful, for preference. A little cottage, perhaps.
Bill All right. You look for something . . .
Kate And then?
Bill I'll find the deposit and then pay the mortgage on it. (*Pause*) It's the best solution, Kate. (*Pause*) What do you say?

There is a pause

Kate (*considering*) No, I don't think so, Bill.
Bill Why not? It comes to the same thing.
Kate I'd be dependent on you in perpetuity or as near as makes no difference. You could have a heart attack, or an accident—or die of cirrhosis of the liver.
Bill I'd take out insurance in your favour.
Kate No. I don't like it. I'd rather have a lump sum and be responsible for my own finances.
Bill There's nothing else on offer. Income, yes, anything within reason. Capital, can't be done. I'm overstretched, too many commitments.
Kate Bill, I can't be held to ransom because of your somewhat over hasty decision to take on a second wife.
Bill I'm not talking about Lucy. (*He points to the telephone*) You heard. A new engine. Do you know how much that'll cost?
Kate Engines do wear out, I'm given to understand. Don't you make some provision for that?
Bill When you get smart, I could hit you, sometimes, Kate.
Kate I know, Bill.
Bill I'm trying to point out that the next few months are going to be difficult, thanks to that bloody engine. That's a fact I can do nothing about.
Kate Bill, dear, that is your little local difficulty, not mine.

Bill Oh, yes it is. It means there's no cash for any modest little tasteful cottage.

Kate Then we're back to selling this one.

Bill Out of the question. And that's final.

Lucy Bill, surely there's another way you haven't mentioned——

Bill There's no other way, Lucy. I thought I'd made that plain. (*He turns to Kate*) Kate, I'm going to ask you again——

Lucy (*interrupting, a flash of anger*) Don't exclude me, please. I think this concerns me too.

Bill (*immediately contrite*) Yes, of course, I'm sorry. Go on.

Lucy I know you've been here a long time—it's been your home, but it's *your* home, yours and Kate's. You bought it together, you furnished it together . . .

Kate Not together, dear. Just me. He was too busy.

Lucy (*to Bill*) It's your home, but it's not mine.

Bill It will be, darling. You'll make it yours.

Lucy I don't really want to tinker about with Kate's ideas. Improve on what she's done.

Kate Tinker, yes. Improve, no. I think not.

Lucy (*to Bill*) We're starting a new life. Shouldn't it be in *our* home? We don't need all this space. We could move to somewhere smaller. And cheaper. Then we'd have our home, and you'd have enough left over for Kate's house.

Kate Case proven, I think. Thank you Lucy.

Bill It wouldn't work.

Kate Why not?

Bill (*to Lucy*) Later on, perhaps. But not now. Trust me, please.

Lucy I'd still like to know your reasons.

Tom Yes. So would I.

Bill When the market improves, we'll sell it then. The more we get the better for everyone—including Kate.

Kate I'm afraid I'm not prepared to wait on your pleasure.

Bill You'll have to. You've no choice.

Kate No? As I understand it, if we can't agree, the court could make an order in effect forcing you to sell.

Bill You do that and you'll get nothing.

Kate Don't be absurd.

Bill I'm telling you, after everything was paid off, nothing.

Kate What utter nonsense. Houses were a lot cheaper when we bought this place, and the mortgage must be nearly paid off by now.

Bill The mortgage. Dear God. If only that was all.

Kate Then what else, Bill?

Bill Capital, that's what. Nearly every business runs on borrowed capital, including mine. Sometimes, you need a fresh injection, just to keep afloat.

Kate Your business is a limited company. A separate entity in law. You told me that.

Bill Banks need security.

Kate Even I know that. The company's asset's the aircraft.

Bill The company assets weren't enough. I had to give a personal guarantee.
Kate Against what?
Tom This house, at a guess. Right, Bill? A second mortgage on this house?
Kate A second mortgage?

Bill nods

How much is paid off?
Bill When the engine's paid for, approximately bugger all.
Kate I see. (*She looks around*) Just a house of cards.
Bill It'll stand. I've worked my way out of bad times before. I can do it
again. But if you go for that court order, school fees, houses, mainten-
ance, forget it. So it's in your own interests to keep me going. Hold off.
Take what's on offer. There's nothing else.
Tom Kate, is this house in both your names?
Kate (*absently*) I think so. Yes.
Tom I'm pretty certain the bank would have insisted on your signature. A
form of consent, something like that.
Kate Yes. Yes, that's right. (*To Bill*) I should have signed something.
Bill You did.
Kate Oh, no.
Bill Check with the bank. You signed.
Kate No. Not knowingly. Not if I knew what I was signing.
Bill I explained it to you.
Kate No, Bill.
Bill It's five, six years ago now. You've forgotten.
Kate I wouldn't forget that. My own home? Oh, no.
Bill (*hard, anger showing*) You signed, Kate. You agreed. It's done.
Lucy Bill, if Kate understood what she was signing—why——
Bill (*interrupting*) Don't ask me what goes on in Kate's mind. She may not
have listened, but she was told, in detail.
Kate I was told nothing. One of your dark little secrets, I suppose.
Tom What does that mean? He's done this sort of thing before?
Bill Done what? She knew, damn it, she knew.
Lucy If so, why would she suggest selling this house?
Bill She can't remember? She doesn't choose to remember? Who knows?
About Kate? I don't. Nothing.
Kate If you had the grace or courage to admit what you did, I wouldn't
mind so much.
Bill What I did kept Sarah at school, and you in the style you enjoy. You
didn't "mind" that did you!
Lucy (*to Bill*) Stop shouting, please and tell me something.
Bill She knew all about it.
Lucy But until this moment, I didn't. Were you hiding it from me?
Bill No, it wasn't like that ...
Lucy We've talked about the house.
Tom That's right, I brought it up.
Lucy You didn't mention any of this.

Bill Women don't understand these things. They get worked up about nothing.

Lucy I'm not a category, I'm not plural, I'm the one you're supposed to want to marry, and love so much you can't tell me.

Bill I do, Lucy.

Lucy Yet you feel you must keep the truth from me? Bill, if I'm not fit to share your problems, including money problems, I don't think I want that.

Bill I keep telling you, there's nothing I can't handle, if only that woman . . . (*He turns to Kate*) If you came to find out how much you can get, now you know.

Kate Very little, it seems. Whatever you choose to dole out.

Bill Oh, you'll be kept in reasonable comfort, Kate. Provided you face reality, because if you don't, I'm finished, and you'll find yourself on social security. I don't think you'd like that much.

Kate No. Nor do I like being threatened and bullied.

Bill Stop playing the victim, Kate. I'm trying to be as fair as I can. You go away and think about it. And while you're at it, think again about Sarah.

Kate (*sharply*) Sarah stays with me. That's settled.

Bill You said I'd lose if I applied for custody.

Kate You would.

Bill Sarah's old enough to have an opinion of her own. If the court asked her which of us she'd rather be with, I think I know what she'd say.

Kate You'd put Sarah through an ordeal like that? For your own selfish ends?

Bill As a last resort, yes, I will. Because I believe she'd grow up a better person with us, away from your influence.

Kate Do you hate me so much that you'd try and take my child away from me?

Bill I don't hate you, Kate, but—my selfish ends? That's you, Kate. Self, self, self, first and last, beginning, middle and end. (*Slight pause*) Oh, this is senseless. There's been nothing worth having between us for years. Just leave, Kate, please. Just go.

Kate (*after a brief pause; quietly*) The last time we were in this room together, you were telling me how much you still loved me. You were begging me not to leave you.

There is a longish silence all round

Lucy Begging *you* not to leave *him*?

Kate Oh, I see. There's a revised version. Forget I said anything. It doesn't matter now.

Lucy It matters to me.

Bill Lucy, you can't believe what she says.

Lucy Be quiet, Bill, please.

Bill For God's sake——

Bill is cut off by Tom who moves to him and grips him roughly

Tom Lucy asked you to keep quiet.

Bill (*to Lucy*) I told you what happened——

Tom throws Bill roughly into a chair leaving him shaken and dazed

Tom Don't make me shut you up properly. Kate, you started something. Finish it.

Kate Oh, dear, I'm afraid his attitude hurt me. I heard words come out of my mouth I had no intention of saying.

Lucy But you did.

Kate I know, but—can't we leave it there?

Lucy No.

Kate Well, as you wish. Some long time ago, I realized you two were having an affair.

Lucy You realized?

Kate Yes.

Lucy Bill didn't tell you?

Kate I didn't have to be told. Good heavens.

Lucy How long ago?

Kate Oh, several months.

Lucy Months?

Kate Yes. At first, I suggested he was seeing too much of you. He laughed it off. You were just friends and so on. Later, I tried again. He told me I was imagining things. After another altercation, I said I thought we should separate. Bill stopped denying it, and became very contrite. He didn't want to hurt you, he needed time to end it gently.

Bill has had a lot to drink and is still too dazed to interrupt

He flew a lot for the next few days. (*To Lucy*) Or he was with you. Either way, I hardly saw him. During those few days I realized something, if with great sadness. Not even for Sarah, could I stay with him. And then, that day three weeks ago, Bill came home with a bunch of red roses, full of love and regret. We had both reached our decision—but not one the other wanted. One of those delicate little ironies life is so full of.

Tom Sod's law. Never fails.

Kate (*to Lucy*) Bill said he'd sent you away. That was supposed to impress me, I suppose.

Lucy Another offering.

Kate Another?

Lucy It doesn't matter.

Kate Bill told me how perfect everything would be from now on. I told him I was leaving. He begged me to change my mind. I refused. Then it became ugly, meaningless, awful. I said things I didn't mean. Threw the first thing to hand. Finally, it came to an end as everything does. And that's how it was.

There is a pause

Bill (*dully*) None of it's true. None of it.

Tom Is it all lies, Kate?

Kate If it would help anyone to believe so, do please, by all means.

Lucy (*vaguely*) Well, I suppose . . . (*She picks up her handbag*) I think I'll go home.
Tom I'll drive you.
Lucy No. I want to be on my own.

Bill despairingly pulls himself together, stands up and moves towards Lucy

Bill Lucy, I swear to God. I've told you nothing but the truth.

Tom bars his way, firm but not now unfriendly

Tom Leave it, Bill. She's had enough.
Bill Lucy, I love you, don't go, please . . . At least listen, look at me . . .

Tom pushes him back into the chair

Tom That'll do, Bill. It's over. Finished. You stay there and keep quiet. I don't want to hurt you. (*To Lucy*) Just see you back safely, that's all. I'll doss down somewhere else.

Lucy moves into the hall and puts on her coat

Tom Well, I'll say goodbye and good luck, Kate.
Kate Thank you, Tom. And you.

Tom and Lucy exit

Bill is still sitting in the chair

Kate I wonder if there's any coffee left. (*She picks up her coffee cup and takes it towards the kitchen. She pauses in the lobby, puts the coffee cup on the deep freeze. She returns to Bill*)
Well, Bill, so much for eternal love.
Bill Why did you do that? How could you?
Kate Do what? Show you it was all a silly daydream? And there was Sarah. I had to protect Sarah. You'd have hurt her. For what? Lucy? She wasn't very loyal, was she.

Kate, from behind, puts her arms round Bill, nuzzles his cheek

(*Her tone becomes soft, seductive*) Anyway, cheer up. It should resolve most of your financial difficulties. Perhaps I shall stay the night after all. You won't mind will you? In fact, it might be rather nice, don't you think?

Kate releases Bill and moves towards the hall

Something snaps in Bill. He stands up and goes after her

Bill You bitch.
Kate (*in a normal voice*) Oh, Bill, don't be so . . . (*She turns and sees him; sudden alarm*) Bill!

In his blind anger, Bill grabs hold of Kate, shakes her and throws her away from him forcefully

Kate stumbles on the step, falls into the lobby and crashes into the deep freeze. She lies prone, with only half of her body visible

Bill You evil bitch. (*He turns back into the living-room, and pours whisky into his glass with a hand which is visibly shaking*) Sarah? No. Hurt pride. Vindictiveness. (*Sudden remorse sets in*) Oh, God, I'm sorry, Kate—I've never raised a hand to you, never—I'm sorry . . . (*Receiving no reply, he puts down his glass, and turns back towards the lobby, as he moves*) Come on, I've said I'm sorry . . . (*He looks down into the lobby*) You're not hurt, are you? (*Pause*) Kate? (*He moves to Kate and bends over her. Touching her*) Kate? Kate? (*In horror*) Oh, no—no . . . (*He retreats into the living-room. Both his hands are blood stained. Deep shock more or less neutralizes the alcohol*) God forgive me, what have I done? (*From now on, while he may behave as if he is thinking things out, is not really in his right mind. He becomes aware of the blood on his hands, looks at them in horror, wipes them on his white shirt, transferring blood stains on to the white cotton. His vacant stare finds the telephone. Slowly, he drags himself to the telephone. He hesitates and then in a murmur*) Police. Yes. Police.

Suddenly, the telephone begins to ring and startles Bill. He waits

The telephone continues to ring relentlessly

(*Finally he lifts the receiver; dully*) Hallo . . . Oh, hallo, I . . . (*Less dull*) What letter? . . . (*He looks at Kate's body*) She wrote . . . (*He listens*) What awful things? . . . Darling, don't please, I . . . Yes, she did come, but she's gone . . . (*Alarmed*) Sarah, no, you can't come home now, you mustn't . . . It's not that darling, I shan't be here . . . (*Racked by Sarah's emotion*) Darling, don't cry, please, I want to see you too, but . . . Next weekend? . . . Half term? Is it? I'd forgotten . . . No, it would be lovely to be with you, of course, it would . . . Darling, I'll have to phone you about it . . . A day or two . . . I will somehow, I promise . . . Yes, all right, sweetheart . . . Love you too . . . (*He hangs up and stares into space for a moment*) Sarah. Oh, God. Sarah.

The doorbell rings, loud and prolonged

Bill starts and stands, frozen

The doorbell rings again

There is determined knocking on the door, followed by another ring on the doorbell

Bill crosses into the hall

Who is it?
Taxi Driver (*off; loudly*) Taxi for the station, name of Taylor.
Bill I didn't order a taxi.
Taxi Driver (*off*) Mrs Taylor. I dropped her here. She told me to come back in an hour.
Bill Hang on. Just a minute. (*He moves hurriedly to his jacket, takes out his wallet and extracts a note. He returns to the front door and opens it a little. He passes the note outside, staying out of sight as he does so*) She decided to catch an earlier train. Sorry. Here. For your trouble.

Taxi Driver (*off*) Oh, right mate. Thanks very much.

Bill closes the door and returns to the living-room. Another thought occurs to him. He moves to the telephone lifts the receiver and taps out a five figure number

Bill (*on the phone*) Alan ... Bill ... That freight for Sumburgh, Tuesday ... I shan't be available, something's come up ... Get on to Ted Johnson's outfit, ask them to take it ... That's it ... Right ... (*He hangs up and turns away. Then he fetches Kate's coat from the hall. Slowly, he moves to Kate, and gently covers her body with the coat. Then he stands erect, looking down at Kate*) Forgive me, Kate. There's Sarah. Forgive me.

Black-out

SCENE 2

The same. Two days later. Tuesday. Early morning into early afternoon

The living-room is in darkness, with the curtains drawn. The light in the kitchen is on. Kate's coat and handbag have gone

There is the sound of the power saw off, starting, stopping, starting, stopping, then continuing for a while. Then it stops

After a pause, Bill comes through the kitchen and into the living-room, carrying a basket of logs. He is now dressed in sweater and slacks, not his uniform. He fills the stove with logs and turns the control up to maximum. He has slept little and looks drawn and pale. But his movements are exact as if carrying out some pre-ordained plan in a trance-like, almost composed, state. He moves towards the lobby and switches off the kitchen light

Black-out then gradually daylight shows around the edges of the curtains as:

In the darkness, there is the sound of the power saw off, starting, stopping, for as long as it will hold. Finally, there is silence

The light in the kitchen comes on

After a moment, Bill appears in the kitchen, and enters the living-room. He is carrying a bundle of clothes. The bundle is wrapped in Bill's bloodstained shirt. Methodically, with no haste, Bill feeds them into the stove. He goes into the kitchen, is out of sight for a moment and returns carrying a suitcase. It is very heavy. He sets it down near the stove and goes back into the kitchen out of sight for a moment and returns with another very heavy suitcase, which he sets down beside its fellow. Each weighs about seventy to eighty pounds. Both suitcases are a reasonably light colour. Bill looks round absently, making sure he has forgotten nothing. Satisfied, he crosses to the telephone, taps out the five figure number

Bill (*into the telephone*) Alan . . . Bill . . . The Cessna fuelled up and ready? . . . What? . . . Customs clearance? No, just the Scilly Isles . . . That's right, Colin and Jill . . . Yes, I'm leaving now . . . (*He hangs up and moves into the hall, undoes the door chain, returns to the living-room and moves to the drinks fitment. To steady himself, he pours a small tot of whisky and swallows it in one gulp*)

More or less ready to go, Bill moves, and is about to lift a suitcase, when:

The doorbell rings, a short, sharp ring. Bill stops, aghast, staring towards the darkened hall. The door knocker is used. Followed by another short ring on the doorbell. Bill remains motionless. And then, to his horror, he hears the front door being unlocked and opened

Daylight appears in the hall

Tom (*off*) Well, his car's in the drive.

Tom appears in the hall, talking to someone outside

You hang on there for a minute. I'll see. (*He pushes the front door to, switches on the living-room lights and enters the living-room. He is surprised to find Bill waiting there*) Hallo. Didn't you hear the bell?
Bill (*indicating the kitchen*) I was outside.
Tom Kate's gone, has she?
Bill Sunday. Soon after you left.
Tom God, you do like it tropical in here, don't you. Curtains still closed as well. Do you know it's two o'clock in the afternoon? Are you all right?
Bill Yes, I——
Tom You don't look it.
Bill A bit tired.
Tom Not sleeping too well, eh?
Bill Look, Tom, I——
Tom Lucy and me, we've been talking. About Sunday. She needs to get something straightened out.
Bill Tom, whatever it is, I can't talk now. Another time.
Tom (*eyeing the suitcases*) You going somewhere?
Bill I need a break, so——
Tom This won't take long.

Tom moves into the hall and speaks to Lucy outside

Bill watches helplessly. He has lost control of events

He is here, love. Come on in.

Lucy appears and enters the living-room

Tom closes the front door and follows her into the living-room

Lucy Hallo Bill. No need to ask how you are. Sunday must have been pretty awful for you.

Bill Yes.

Lucy (*registering the suitcases*) Oh, you're going away. Where? To stay with Colin and Jill?

Bill Yes.

Lucy There's something I——

Bill (*interrupting*) Not now, Lucy. I'm sorry, but I must go.

Tom If you're flying your own plane, it's not going to leave without you, is it.

Bill no longer has the stamina to resist

Lucy Tom hasn't been staying at the house—but we've talked . . .

Bill He said.

Lucy We've discussed—starting again . . . Tom thinks we should but there was real love between us, you and me . . . I thought there was—until Sunday. I can't answer Tom—until—there's something I need to know first . . .

Bill What is it you need to know, Lucy?

Lucy It was all too emotional—I didn't really give you a chance—you said Kate wasn't speaking the truth. And I've thought since, it could have been spite. Or malice. Or jealousy. Was it? Tell me Bill, please.

Bill There was real love, Lucy. There was. You can believe that. But you must also believe that every word Kate said was true. I can't explain. That's your answer. I'm sorry.

Lucy Thank you. (*She turns away from both of them*) That's what I had to know.

Tom You want to collect your clothes and stuff?

Lucy Not now. I'd like to go home, please.

Tom (*to Bill*) Some other time, OK?

Bill Yes.

Tom leads Lucy to the front door. It looks as if they are going

You wait in the car, love. I just want a quick word with Bill.

Lucy exits

Tom closes the front door after Lucy and comes back into the living-room

Bill Tom. Please——

Tom Bill, is there anything you'd like to tell me, you wouldn't want to say in front of Lucy?

Bill I don't know what you mean.

Tom There's something off key. Like you not wanting to answer the door. Waiting here in the dark.

Bill I told you, I——

Tom And what are you doing here, anyway? We came round to push a note through the door, from Lucy. (*He shows Bill the note*) Saw your car. Thought perhaps you were ill or something. You were supposed to be flying to Sumburgh.

Bill I couldn't face it—the long flight . . .

Tom You're flying to the Scilly Isles. With enough luggage for a month by the look of it. When are you coming back?

Bill I don't know—after everything that's happened—this house—whether I could ever bear to see it again—I don't know.

Tom Because of Lucy? Are you saying she's the reason?

Bill Lucy, Kate, everything. Lucy's back where she belongs. Leave it at that.

Tom Lucy took what you said one way. I took it another. You didn't actually say Kate was speaking the truth on Sunday. Only that Lucy must *believe* she was. Was Kate lying or wasn't she?

Bill If you believe something, it's true, isn't it?

Tom Kate was very convincing. She convinced me.

Bill She could adjust reality. Re-arrange hurtful events in her mind. We all do it to some extent. Kate more than most. Did she know in her heart? I could never tell. It's how she was. Human, like the rest of us.

Tom You're very reluctant to blame Kate, all of a sudden.

Bill I can't go back and change anything. It's too late.

Tom Why? If you'd told Lucy that Kate was lying, she might have stayed with you. Instead, you contrive a form of words that puts her outside, waiting for me. It doesn't fit. Something's not right.

Bill Let me go, Tom. If I don't leave soon, it'll be too late.

Tom Too late for what?

Bill The airport in the Scilly Isles—they won't accept fixed wing aircraft after dark. Let me go.

Tom Bill, I wish you no harm. We were good friends once. If there's anything I can do, anything at all . . .

Bill Take Lucy home. Be good to her. You can do that.

Tom Well, think it over. The offer stands. Safe trip and all that. (*He makes to go and then remembers something and turns back*) Oh, Lucy's key. (*He bends to place the key on the coffee table*)

Blood begins to ooze down one of the suitcases

Tom holds the bent position for a long moment as he now sees what Bill sees at about the same time—oozing through the join between lid and suitcase at the top of one of the suitcases and beginning to ooze down the side is blood

Tom straightens up slowly, and meets Bill's eyes

(*Shaken*) Dear God—so—that's why . . .

The blood is continuing to ooze

Tom recovers with an effort and adopts a "professional" tone. He half lifts the suitcase which is not "bleeding". It is a considerable effort

Lead weights, right? It could have worked. Sitting on the sea bed off Lands End, quietly rotting. (*He crouches and examines the oozing blood*) Contents wrapped in plastic bags I'm sure. One of them must have split.

Bill sits down, shattered—reality is beginning to return

When did it happen?

Bill Sunday. It was an accident. I pushed her. She fell. I didn't mean to kill her.

Tom Then why didn't you call the police, Bill? Why this?

Bill It was Sarah—she phoned ... Kate had written—Sarah waited until she thought Kate would have left—she just wanted to see me—me—and I couldn't bear to tell her—for her to know—and I thought—I'll take her abroad ... We'll live there ... There was nothing I could do for Kate—it sounds insane, now—now, I can't believe—the things I've done ...

There is a pause

Tom (*indicating the telephone*) Shall I phone?

Bill No. No. (*He stands, moves to the telephone and taps in nine, nine, nine. Speaks into the phone; a flat unemotional tone*) Police ... (*Pause*) My name is William Taylor. Address, 'Fairview', the name of the house, Oxford Road. Telephone number five-six-nine-two-three. My wife is dead. I killed her. I'm at the house now. (*He hangs up*)

CURTAIN

FURNITURE AND PROPERTY LIST

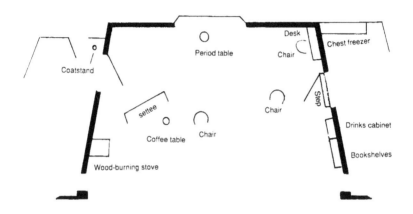

ACT I

Scene 1

On stage: Large deep freeze (in lobby)
Coatstand (in hall)
Wood-burning stove
Curtains at bay window
Settee
Two armchairs
Coffee table
Small period table. *On it:* vase. *In it:* wilting flowers
Desk. *On it:* typewriter or small word processor, telephone, notepad, pen, address book
Desk chair
Well-stocked bookshelves
Drinks fitment. *In it:* glasses, bottles of sherry, whisky, Martini, gin and wine

Off stage: Basket. *In it:* newly sawn logs **(Bill)**

Scene 2

Strike: Logs from the store
Wilted flowers
Used glasses

Set: Fresh flowers in vase
                Open curtains
                Fresh glasses

Off stage: Briefcase **(Bill)**
                Shopping bag **(Lucy)**

Personal: **Bill:** Pilot's cap
                Tom: Watch

SCENE 3

Personal: **Kate:** Handbag

ACT II

SCENE 1

Strike: Logs from the basket
                Used glasses

Set: Fresh glasses
                Blood capsules in the lobby

Off stage: Cup of coffee **(Lucy)**
                Basket full of logs **(Bill)**

Personal: **Bill:** Wallet. *In it:* five pound note

SCENE 2

Strike: **Kate's** coat and handbag
                Log basket
                Coffee cup on freezer

Off stage: Basket full of logs **(Bill)**
                Bill's blood-stained shirt wrapped around a bundle of clothes **(Bill)**
                Two heavy light-coloured suitcases **(Bill)**

Personal: **Tom:** note and key

LIGHTING PLOT

Property fittings required: stove with glow effect

Interior. The same scene throughout

ACT I, SCENE 1.   Early evening

To open: General interior lighting in the living-room and from the hall.
Cold, hard fluorescent light from the kitchen. Glow from
stove

Cue 1   **Bill:** "Nothing to be afraid of. Nothing."   (Page 9)
Fade to Black-out

ACT I, SCENE 2.   Late afternoon

To open: Winter evening exterior lighting through bay window

Cue 2   Front door opens   (Page 9)
Exterior light through the door frame

Cue 3   **Bill** switches on the hall light   (Page 9)
Hall light on

Cue 4   **Bill** switches on the living-room lights   (Page 9)
Living-room lights on

Cue 5   **Tom** exits out of sight and silently lets himself out (Page 20)
Fade to Black-out

ACT I, SCENE 3.   Afternoon

To open: Dull November afternoon. Exterior lighting through the bay
window. Fluorescent light from the kitchen

Cue 6   **Tom:** "—somehow we weren't expecting to see you either, (Page 25)
Kate."
Black-out

ACT II, SCENE 1.   Afternoon

To open: As in previous scene but with the exterior lighting fading
throughout the scene

Cue 7   **Bill** switches on lights   (Page 32)
General interior lighting

Cue 8   **Bill:** "Forgive me"   (Page 42)
Black-out

ACT II, SCENE 2.   Early morning to late afternoon

To open: Fluorescent light from the kitchen

Cue 9	**Bill** moves towards the lobby and switches off the kitchen light	(Page 42)
	Black-out then gradually daylight shows around the edges of the curtains	

Cue 10	When ready	(Page 42)
	Light in the kitchen comes on	

Cue 11	Front door opens	(Page 43)
	Daylight appears in the hall through the open door	

Cue 12	**Tom** switches on the living-room lights	(Page 43)
	General interior lighting	

EFFECTS PLOT

PROLOGUE

Cue 1   As House Lights dim   (Page vi)
           Pre-recorded dialogue (as page vi) on tape

ACT I

SCENE 1

Cue 2   As the CURTAIN rises   (Page 1)
           Rasping, intermittent snarl of a power saw off stage

Cue 3   **Bill** exits into the kitchen   (Page 2)
           Sound of running water

Cue 4   **Lucy** begins to move towards her coat   (Page 6)
           Telephone rings

Cue 5   **Lucy** exits into the kitchen   (Page 7)
           Sound of a fridge door opening, a pause, then closing again

Cue 6   To open SCENE 2   (Page 9)
           Car stops outside. Engine is switched off. Door slams

Cue 7   **Bill** moves to the stove absentmindedly   (Page 10)
           Different car door slams and footsteps are heard on the path

Cue 8   **Lucy:** "How I ever lived with you—just get out."   (Page 20)
           Telephone rings

Cue 9   **Lucy** opens the deep freeze and looks inside   (Page 21)
           Prolonged ring on the front door bell

Cue 10   **Lucy:** "—to remember that awful murder you brought up ..."   (Page 24)
           Telephone rings

ACT II

Cue 11   **Bill:** "Yes. Police."   (Page 41)
           Telephone rings

Cue 12   **Bill:** "Oh God, Sarah."   (Page 41)
           Doorbell rings, loud and prolonged. Again

Cue 13   To open SCENE 2   (Page 42)
           Sound of a power saw starting and stopping

Cue 14   **Bill** moves and is about to lift a suitcase, when;   (Page 43)
           Doorbell rings, a short, sharp ring

Cue 15   The door knocker is used   (Page 43)
           Short ring on the door bell

MADE AND PRINTED IN GREAT BRITAIN BY
LATIMER TREND & COMPANY LTD PLYMOUTH

MADE IN ENGLAND